COME LET US
Adore Him

A HIGHLY FAVOURED CHRISTMAS DEVOTIONAL

Copyright © The Highly Favoured Life 2024

Published and Designed by Unmovable Publications

ALL RIGHTS RESERVED
to The Highly Favoured Life and authorized writers.

No part of this book may be reproduced, transmitted, or sold in any form or by any means, electronic, or mechanical, including photocopying, recording, or by any information storage and retrieval system, without permission in writing from the publisher.

All scripture quotations are from
the King James Version (KJV) of the Bible.

ISBN:
9798339518310 (paperback)
9798339518372 (hardback)

Table of Contents

Most Wonderful Time of Year 7
By Julianna Young

The Three Wise Women 11
By Susan Hutchens

The Fullness of Christmastime 17
By Candance Voyles

The Greatest Gift 21
By Hannah Suttle

Lessons Learned from Mary's Responses (Part 1) . . . 27
By Hope Reimers

Lessons Learned from Mary's Responses (Part 2) . . . 35
By Hope Reimers

Joseph – A Man of Notable Character (Part 1) . . . 41
By Kelly Byrley

Joseph – A Man of Notable Character (Part 2) . . . 47
By Kelly Byrley

How Should A King Come? 53
By Larissa Bell

When Christmas Doesn't Look the Same 59
By Rainy Lehman

God's Christmas Plan 65
By Breanna Patton

God Chooses to Use Small 69
By Lydia L. Riley

The Highly Favoured Hard Life 75
    By Deborah South

Home for the Holidays. 81
    By Nicole Redmon

Two Kings - King Herod and King Jesus 87
    By Makayla Fehr

The Most Wonderful Time of the Year 93
    By Kate Ledbetter

Growing with God 97
    By Cherith Shiflett

Christmas Joy 103
    By Renee Patton

The Gift That Keeps On Giving 109
    By Bethany Riley

Let Every Heart Prepare Him Room 115
    By Callie Payne

The Gift of the Present (Part 1) 119
    By Kathy Lane

The Gift of the Present (Part 2) 125
    By Kathy Lane

It's a Wonderful Life! 129
    By Debra Birner

Will You Submit? 133
    By Grace Shiflett

The Joy the Saviour Brought 137
    By Rikki Beth Poindexter

Introduction

Ah, it's beginning to look a lot like Christmas. The sights and sounds of this beautiful season fill many of us with the warmth of love and giving. For others, this season comes on the hills of a tragedy or painful reminder of past loss and hurts. For some, this season is spent counting their pennies to afford a small treat for their loved ones. Some may be spending Christmas far from family and friends, striving to make new memories but silently longing to be closer to home.

While some churches prepare for Christmas party after Christmas party, some churches are left without a pastor this season. While some ladies may be baking the days away for their gift-giving, others are rushing from store to store with coupons to get the best deals possible. Grandmas are spending far too much on grandbabies. Wives are feverishly writing their Christmas list ideas for their husbands. Mothers are planning a Christmas feast in one house, while another mother is trying to get off a few hours early on Christmas day. Single ladies are diligently wrapping gifts for family members. A new Christian mother is learning how to incorporate the nativity in her yearly decor while a senior saint of God is slowly unwrapping the fragile heirloom nativity set she has displayed for years.

No matter which one of these ladies you are, you can have a joyful season. Christ's gift to us shines extra bright this season amid the hustle and bustle, the sorrow and pain, the uncertainty or questions... So take a few minutes every day to prepare your heart to see Jesus this Christmas. Be reminded of Him. Seek ways to show your adoration. And just as you would unwrap your favorite gift in the whole world, unwrap His love for you and seek to adore Him more and more every day.

Merry Christmas!

Most Wonderful Time of Year

By Julianna Young

But Mary kept all these things, and pondered them in her heart.
Luke 2:19

I absolutely love Christmas! If you would've asked me a couple years ago what I liked about Christmas, I would've told you my favorite part was the traditions — the baking, the decorating, the gift-wrapping.... It is all so much fun to me! As I have gotten older, that answer has changed.

I was saved at a very young age, but I felt as if I would always get caught up in the activities and festivities of Christmas rather than taking a step back to truly appreciate what Christmas is all about. It wasn't until I was about nineteen that I truly started enjoying Christmas and the true meaning of it.

That year, I was encouraged to do a scripture writing plan through the month of December. Each day of the month was spent reading a portion of scripture dealing with our Savior's birth and things surrounding that wonderful event. As I saturated myself in the Word every day in December, I couldn't help but constantly meditate on the story of Christmas. It truly sent me into a spirit of thankfulness that entire month. I remember as my Dad was reading Luke 2 to me and my siblings on Christmas morning, I just sat there and tears began to fill my eyes. As we prayed before we opened presents, I was just thanking the Lord over and over for sending His Son to be born in a manger and to die for me! I know for a fact that because I decided to take a step back that year and focus on the true meaning of Christmas, it made that year one that I will always remember!

I want to encourage you to do the same. I have compiled some of my favorite passages concerning Jesus' birth and divided it into 25 days. You can read a passage each day and then even write it down in a notebook to meditate on if you would like. I hope we all spend this month saturating ourselves in the true meaning of Christmas and the reason why we celebrate the season. It truly is the most wonderful time of the year!

- ☐ Day 1 - Isaiah 7:14
- ☐ Day 2 - Isaiah 9:6-7
- ☐ Day 3 - Luke 1:26-28
- ☐ Day 4 - Luke 1:29-31
- ☐ Day 5 - Luke 1:32-33
- ☐ Day 6 - Luke 1:34-35
- ☐ Day 7 - Luke 1:36-38
- ☐ Day 8 - Luke 1:39-41
- ☐ Day 9 - Luke 1:42-45
- ☐ Day 10 - Luke 1:46-48
- ☐ Day 11 - Luke 1:49-51
- ☐ Day 12 - Luke 1:52-53
- ☐ Day 13 - Luke 1:54-56
- ☐ Day 14 - Matthew 1:18-20
- ☐ Day 15 - Matthew 1:21-23
- ☐ Day 16 - Matthew 1:24-25
- ☐ Day 17 - Luke 2:7
- ☐ Day 18 - Luke 2:8-10
- ☐ Day 19 - Luke 2:11-12
- ☐ Day 20 - Luke 2:13-14
- ☐ Day 21 - Luke 2:15-16
- ☐ Day 22 - Luke 2:17-20
- ☐ Day 23 - Matthew 2:1-2
- ☐ Day 24 - Matthew 2:3-6
- ☐ Day 25 - Matthew 2:7-11

COME LET US Adore Him

Thoughts

How I Adore Him

The Three Wise Women

By Susan Hutchens

And Mary said, Behold the handmaid of the Lord;
be it unto me according to thy word...

Luke 1:38

In the account of Jesus' birth and early years in Luke 1-2, we read about the visit of, what we refer to as, "the three wise men." We don't really know that there were specifically three wise men, of course; we take that thought from the three gifts they brought to the young child Jesus.

Having said that, we do know for certain that there were three women associated with the birth and first days of Jesus' life: Elisabeth, the cousin of Jesus' mother; Mary, Jesus' mother; and Anna, a devoted woman anticipating the birth of the Messiah. I like to call these the "Three Wise Women of Jesus' Birth." Each of these women was very different from one another.

Elisabeth was a wife of many years in "the ministry" as the wife of a priest and of the priestly line herself. She was at least middle-aged because she was past her child-bearing years (Luke 1:5-7). Mary, the mother of Jesus, was a single young woman, most likely an older teenager, and of the honored tribe of Judah through which the

"I have one desire now - to live a life of reckless abandon for the Lord, putting all my energy and strength into it."

- Elisabeth Elliot

Messiah would come (Luke 1:26-27). Anna was very old. She'd been a widow for eighty-four years, having only been married for seven years. If we add to those ninety-one years about fourteen years or so as the age she may have married, we can see that she was probably over 105 years old! Anna was of the tribe of Asher, one of the "forgotten tribes." Maybe she was not considered a descendant of a very important family (Luke 2:36-37).

Each of these women was known for her character.

Elisabeth was a supportive woman. We see that she supported her husband when everyone questioned him (Luke 1:59-63). She also supported Mary when Mary came to her as an unwed, pregnant teenager. I would imagine that almost everyone else in Mary's life was anything but supportive. But Elisabeth, being a spirit-filled woman, realized that the baby Mary was carrying was the long-awaited Messiah and became the first woman to praise the Lord Jesus (Luke 1:41-42)!

Mary was a surrendered woman. One of my favorite verses in the Bible was spoken by Mary: "Behold the handmaid of the Lord: be it unto me according to thy word" (Luke 1:38). Just to read a bit between the lines, Mary may have wondered how she was going to explain this pregnancy to her parents, family, and friends, especially to Joseph. She probably realized life was not going to be easy for her during the pregnancy; she would lose friends, lose respect in the community, and maybe lose her fiance and his love. But even as she knew these things may happen, she surrendered herself to God's plan. And even though she didn't understand how everything would turn out, she surrendered herself in faith, believing God's Word.

Lastly, Anna was a separated woman. She wasn't just outwardly separated. Yes, she was always at the temple (perhaps lived there) and fasted and prayed night and day (Luke 2:37). Everyone knew how separated she was! But she also had to have been dedicated to God from her heart, because she was familiar with the scriptural prophecies and recognized that the baby Jesus was the Messiah she had been waiting for. She had a good relationship with God and knew His Word as the basis of her outward separation.

As I live each day, I want to be a supportive woman. I want to support my husband and children, my extended family, and my friends through God's promises in His Word, as Elisabeth did. I'd also love to be a surrendered woman like Mary. I want to make it my practice to daily surrender to God's will, without question or complaint, even without necessarily understanding. I want to trust Him! And I'd like to be a separated woman, not just outwardly, but more importantly, separated to God inwardly, dwelling with Him through His Word and prayer. Will you join these three wise women in their support, surrender, and separation to the Lord?

COME LET US Adore Him

Thoughts

How I Adore Him

The Fullness of Christmastime

By Candance Voyles

But when the fulness of time was come, God sent forth his Son, made of a woman, made under the law, To redeem them that were under the law, that we might receive the adoption of sons.

Galatians 4:4-5

Christmas just has its own special magic and meaning for all those who celebrate it. There are so many memories and moments we associate with it – from the decorations, the time spent with family, to the wonder of the children and seeing Christmas through their eyes. Most special of all is the birth of the Son of God into this world. That is what means the most to those of us who know the Lord and have been redeemed.

To so many, myself included, Christmas can also be a difficult time of year. When you have experienced grief, loss, or pain. When someone, especially a child, is missing around the table, those memories can bring more hurt than joy. The tasks that once you enjoyed at this time of year can become overwhelming. One thing remains the same through it all— Emmanuel, God with us. It really does strip this time of year down to the basics. In our hearts, we can rejoice in that fact. He came to where we are to feel our hurts and to take our sorrows and our sins so that we would never be alone again.

The phrase in this verse jumped out at me— "the fulness of time." Since my little boy went to heaven, I have often thought about time — how it is both cruel and merciful to me now. It ebbs and flows like the tide. From the time we are born, we begin to die. Death is our natural enemy. Every moment I look at my children getting older, I watch time slip away so fast.

I feel the time since I last saw Jack's smiling face. It feels so long ago. But there was a moment in history when time was at its fullest. It was at its most merciful to mankind and cruelest to the Son of God because He came to take away and become our sin. He came to die.

Even though loss and difficulties can tarnish some of the brightness of the season we call "the most wonderful time of the year," we can also look at it in this Light. This Light is the fulness of time — for all time, as well as this time of year. It is everything and all things that He would come to where we are. No wonder there was "glory to God in the highest" and could be "peace on earth and goodwill toward men!"

Jesus is with us and will never leave nor forsake us. Because the "fulness of time" came, our joy can still be full today, no matter what we may face.

COME LET US Adore Him

Thoughts

How I Adore Him

The Greatest Gift

By Hannah Suttle

For unto us a child is born, unto us a son is given: and the government shall be upon his shoulder: and his name shall be called Wonderful, Counsellor, The mighty God, The everlasting Father, The Prince of Peace.

Isaiah 9:6

With Christmas quickly approaching, many ideas come through the mind. Maybe for those that plan well in advance, spring or summer are the months that you get your Christmas shopping done. Maybe you're the one who goes shopping on Black Friday to get all the special deals. Or maybe, you're the one that goes shopping at 8pm on Christmas Eve, trying your best to pull together a special gift for one that you love. No matter when you go shopping, giving requires personal sacrifice. You spend your hard-earned money and some of your precious time to make sure that person has a wonderful holiday. Your end goal is not just to have a gift under the Christmas tree but rather to let that person know how very much they're loved.

The purpose of Jesus' death on the cross is not just to have a gift to offer, but to let you know how much He loves you.

Today, friend, I would like to quickly share with you the greatest gift that I ever received. There was a Vacation Bible School at our church in the morning and a Teen Connection in the evening. I was a six-year-old pastor's daughter, so no matter what the church event, I was there. Our church served the teenagers dinner after the service each evening. My job while my parents ran Teen Connection was to assist the ladies in the kitchen, opening chip bags, setting out silverware, etc. I loved this job, especially since I got to go play outside afterwards. Well, it was a Wednesday, and my mom told me that I needed to go to the teen service instead of helping out in the kitchen. I did not want to go and had a bad attitude about it. But thank the Lord for a mom who made me go to church! That night, the preacher preached on sin and its consequences – an eternal hell, a lake burning with fire and brimstone, eternal damnation. I'd heard it all before, but it had never felt so pointed. He named several sins that I wasn't worried about and then said, "Even having a rebellious spirit against your parents will send you to hell." I distinctly remember the immediate conviction that followed. Suddenly, all the things I'd ever done wrong flooded back to my memory. I couldn't escape the thought that hell was going to be my eternal home if I died that night. Sure, I was only six and never committed adultery or murder. But the Bible said my lies and bad attitude were enough to send me to hell (Romans 6:23, Revelation 21:8)!

Gratefully, the message didn't stop there. He went on to explain how God loved me so very much: He sent His only Son Jesus to die on the cross for my sins (Romans 5:8). He explained that I don't have to work for my salvation or makeup for all of my sins in any way (Ephesians 2:8-9), but simply believe that Jesus is God, repent of my sins, and ask Jesus to save me of my sins (Romans 10:9, I John 1:9). Jesus loved me so much that He made the ultimate personal sacrifice to give me an eternity in Heaven, and all I had to do was accept His gift of salvation (Romans 10:13). On June 19, 2005, I accepted God's wonderful gift of salvation. That was the very best day of my life; there has never been a day that I regretted it!

I believe I would be deceived to think that each person reading this book has accepted God's gift of salvation. Dear friend, I beg you today, that if you haven't asked Jesus to be your personal Savior, do that today! The purpose of Jesus' death on the cross is not just to have a gift to offer, but to let you know how much He loves you. We are not promised tomorrow, so please do not put it off! It will be the best decision you ever make, and the greatest gift you ever receive!

COME LET US Adore Him

Thoughts

How I Adore Him

Lessons Learned from Mary's Responses
(Part 1)

By Hope Reimers

For with God nothing shall be impossible.
Luke 1:37

The Christmas story is one of the most well-known stories in existence. I'd be lying if I didn't say there haven't been times it has lost some of its luster after years of hearing this story repetitively in the same way. There were a few things I noticed looking through Mary's perspective that changed the view I had of the great Christmas story. We know it was absolutely a divine miracle, but there is also quite a bit of humanity that makes this story so much more real and applicable to Christians now.

Mary's Reaction to the News

Luke 1:28 - "And the angel came in unto her, and said, Hail, thou that art highly favoured, the Lord is with thee: blessed art thou among women." In my vivid imagination, Gabriel, the angel, is probably quite excited to be given the task to deliver news that will change the world, so when he gets to Mary, he greets her with that same excitement. "Hello! Oh, you are so favoured! God is with you, and you're one of the most blessed women to ever exist!" *smile* Now, Mary's reaction on the other hand was not, "Wow! Me?!" It was more like, "Who are you? What are you doing in my house, and what kind of greeting was that?" In her mind, she understandably could have thought, "You're talking like you've known me for a while, but you never even introduced yourself or told me from where you traveled."

Luke 1:29 - "And when she saw him, she was troubled at his saying, and cast in her mind what manner of salutation this should be." In the next few verses, Gabriel backtracks and tries again telling her not to be afraid and that she will soon be pregnant with a son named Jesus who will reign over a forever kingdom. What I found interesting is the fact that there is no indication at this point in the conversation that Mary knew she was talking to an angel. All she knows is that a stranger from who-knows-where has come up to her very excitedly telling her that she is going to be pregnant.

Mary's Rejection of the Truth

Luke 1:34 - "Then said Mary unto the angel, How shall this be, seeing I know not a man?" She was probably doubting this person with the unbelievable news and trying to find a way to dismiss him so that she could get back to finishing her work for the day. Then in verse 35, the angel explains that she will conceive by the Holy Ghost and give birth to that holy Thing, who will be called the Son of God. Next, what the angel says in verse 36 is when I believe the truth starts to solidify in her mind.

Luke 1:36 - "And, behold, thy cousin Elisabeth, she hath also conceived a son in her old age: and this is the sixth month with her, who was called barren." The initial news of Mary conceiving just didn't make much sense logically, but now Gabriel brought up her cousin. I imagine Mary started to realize that this person very well would have spoken the truth if he also knew about this other family miracle. The angel also ended with this powerful statement.

Luke 1:37 - "For with God nothing shall be impossible." I don't think there was much Mary could say after hearing this "stranger" say, "For with God nothing shall be impossible."

__Mary's Resignation to the Truth__

Luke 1:38 - "And Mary said, Behold the handmaid of the Lord; be it unto me according to thy word. And the angel departed from her." Mary believed and accepted the truth. She acknowledged that she is a servant of the Lord and that whatever He willed would happen. What I found missing from Luke 1:26-38 is that it never once mentions Mary being happy about this situation. She believed the news was real, but to her initially, it probably wasn't a blessing.

She may have started in doubt, but she ended in belief.

She might have seen it as a trial. "If this is true, what will my fiancé think of me? What about my friends, my family? Will they believe me when I try to explain what happened?" I can't help but think there was at least one time when she didn't think or feel like she was "blessed" as the angel said.

Mary's Realization of the Truth

Mary went straight to her cousin Elisabeth's house because she was the one person this "stranger" mentioned in that shocking conversation. She just needed someone to talk to who could possibly understand what was happening. She knew Elisabeth's husband was a priest, and Elisabeth was a pastor's wife, so maybe they could help shed light on the situation. Even before Mary could start to talk about what just happened between her and the angel, God steps in and speaks through Elisabeth to Mary and repeats some of the angel's words loudly.

Luke 1:41-42 And it came to pass, that when Elisabeth heard the salutation of Mary, the babe leaped in her womb; and Elisabeth was filled with the Holy Ghost: And she spake with a loud voice, and said, Blessed art thou among women, and blessed is the fruit of thy womb.

"Blessed art thou among women." It was no accident God repeated that message and those exact words the angel previously told her. When God says something once, He means it, but when God says something twice, He wants it emphasized. We also probably didn't listen or pay attention the first time, so He needed to repeat it! I can imagine God thinking, "If you didn't fully believe my message from the angel, maybe you'll believe it from your cousin."

"Blessed is the fruit of your womb" Mary probably didn't see this pregnancy as a blessing because she knew how it would affect her reputation. She'd undoubtedly tried to live a good, clean life – God chose her out of all women to be the mother of the Savior!

The angel previously told her in detail why this child would be a blessing, but again God had to repeat that message. Verse 43 is when I think the full weight of the truth started to sink in. Luke 1:43, says, "And whence is this to me, that the mother of my Lord should come to me? Luke 1:45a, says, "And blessed is she that believed:" She may have started in doubt, but she ended in belief.

COME LET US Adore Him

Thoughts

How I Adore Him

Lessons Learned from Mary's Responses
(Part 2)

By Hope Reimers

For with God nothing shall be impossible.
Luke 1:37

Mary's Rejoicing in the Truth

Luke 1:46-55 is verse after verse of Mary praising the Lord for his goodness! I imagine Mary felt overwhelmed with worry at the beginning. Her mind throughout the trip to her cousin's home was most likely filled with questions of how, why, what if, and when? Now, she finally understood and heard the truth through God's perspective. I imagine tears of joy and comfort pouring down while she praised the Lord that He had looked down, saw her, and chose her to be the mother of the world's Saviour. This time, she felt overwhelmed with relief. The doubts and the fears slipped away, and she was able to embrace her situation rather than question it. God didn't change her situation. He helped her change her perspective of the situation.

Finding real joy in trials through the Lord is the Christian's new perspective of trials.

Mary's Reputation Despite the Truth

She was able to rejoice, but her life wasn't always easy. She came back home to a fiancé who doubted her integrity. After about three months of helping Elisabeth, she comes back home pregnant. Joseph loved her but was understandably unsure of the situation, which is why an angel had to come and explain to Joseph that everything was alright, and Mary did nothing wrong. God was able to clear the doubt of Mary's reputation in Joseph's mind, but no record shows God sent an angel or a sign to all of their friends and family to prove her innocence. Mary's reputation may have been tainted in the eyes of people, but she was "highly favoured" by the One Who mattered most. I believe Mary had harsh criticism starting the moment her pregnancy was announced. I'm sure she and her family, including Jesus, were treated differently because some thought He was a child born out of adultery. She may have had critics, but I believe it allowed her to live a life that was pleasing to God rather than men because there was no appeasing critical people.

All of Mary's responses relate to how we respond to situations as Christians.
- Mary's Reaction – Overwhelmed
- Mary's Rejection – Doubt - Every human's immediate response
- Mary's Resignation – "I believe God" with head knowledge. The Christian's response to God's ability – "For with God nothing is impossible." We believe it, but don't always apply it personally. We look for how we can fix it on our own.

- Mary's Realization – "I believe God" with the whole reality and heart knowledge. The Christian's lightbulb moment during preaching, lesson, or devotion. "That message or truth was just for me."
- Mary's Rejoicing – Finding real joy in trials through the Lord is the Christian's new perspective of trials. There is a joy that can be found in trials, but sometimes we're looking in the wrong spot. Sometimes we think the source of our joy is found in things or even people.
- Mary's Reputation - Whether people think we do things for the right reasons or not doesn't always matter. A good reputation is important, but it is not everything, simply because we cannot please everyone.

In conclusion, what are our responses to problems in life? We may start with immediate, rash reactions, but do we end there? Do we take it a couple of steps further, pause, and look wider at the whole reality? Do we take that Bible head knowledge we know so well and apply it personally? Do we see our situation through our own eyes and personal perspective or the eyes of the Lord and His Word?

When we're in a situation that we don't understand at all or don't see the light in our life, I hope we take the time to look directly to the Light Who will guide us through every decision if we let Him.

COME LET US Adore Him

Thoughts

How I Adore Him

Joseph — A Man of Notable Character
(Part 1)

By Kelly Byrley

Then Joseph being raised from sleep did as the angel of the Lord had bidden him, and took unto him his wife:

Matthew 1:24

At Christmas, we should always place the greatest emphasis on the birth of Jesus. His birth is the Christmas story. In that story, Mary's name comes up quite often. How could it not? She was the "highly favoured" virgin whom God chose to miraculously birth His Son. We know that Mary was a righteous young lady who lived in such a way that God noticed her. There are some very important lessons we can learn from a study on Mary, but what about Joseph? Maybe it's just me, but I don't hear Joseph discussed much at all. Although there isn't much written about him in the Bible, there are plenty of valuable little nuggets that can help us as moms and as single ladies.

Joseph possessed some incredible character traits. Just like Mary, he also lived a pure and righteous life. How can we know that without hearing the Lord refer to him as "highly favoroued" or "blessed?" We know this simply because the Lord chose Mary, and she was espoused to Joseph. The Lord knew that Joseph possessed the integrity and character He could trust to be the earthly authority in Jesus' life. God knew that Joseph would lead Mary and the children in his home in the right way.

Why is that important for us as moms and as single ladies? Moms, we need to be instilling these character traits into our sons, as well as teaching our daughters to look for these in a spouse. Single ladies, you need to be looking for these qualities in a man when you are waiting for a spouse. If your children are grown or if you have no children, you can still encourage these traits in other boys and young men in your life. This task isn't just limited to moms.

Before we take a closer look at the character of Joseph, let's look at the customs and traditions surrounding Mary and Joseph's espousal. When two people were espoused, it was much more serious than our engagements today. The espousal was a legally binding contract that recognized two people as married even though they were not able to enjoy all of the things that come with marriage such as intimacy and living together until their marriage was consummated. The only way to break the contract of an espousal was by a bill of divorcement by the husband, usually if the wife had been unfaithful or found not to be a virgin. A husband could even have his wife stoned for being unfaithful. That was a very serious crime. Understanding the customs of the time allows us to better understand Joseph's character as he handled the situation he was facing with Mary. Let's put ourselves in Joseph's shoes for a minute. Mary is a pure, godly young lady. Joseph has also remained pure, lived righteously, and worked hard to prepare a home for him and his new bride. They have no doubt studied the Scriptures, prayed, and worshipped together. Mary is the love of his life. He can't wait for them to truly begin their life together. Then one day he finds out she's expecting. He knows he had no part in that. Mary's been gone for a few months visiting Elizabeth. She says she's innocent. Most likely, she tells him about her visit from the angel. It all seems so unbelievable and overwhelming. He knows Mary and wants to believe her, but he also has common sense, and her story seems impossible to believe. He debates with himself. He's not sure if he should trust her or not. He considers secretly writing her a bill of divorcement. As he is considering these things, the angel speaks to him. Here's where we will pick up our study of his character.

Prudent

Matthew 1:19 describes Joseph's turmoil. I cannot imagine the thoughts and feelings that were overwhelming him. I am sure he was torn in wanting to trust his wife, but wasn't sure he could. We have to remember that we are looking at this as history, but it was happening to Joseph in real time. I am sure he was jealous, angry, hurt, and confused. Yet, he didn't react. He took some time to think about it. Most likely, he prayed about it. He didn't make any rash decisions in the heat of the moment. We can see that he had made walking circumspectly a habit based on how he handled the situation. (Further reading: Ephesians 5:15, Proverbs 18:13, Psalm 94:19, Proverbs 25:28, Proverbs 14:8.)

> Joseph was faithful. He trusted the Lord.
> He obeyed, even when it went against common sense.

COME LET US Adore Him

Thoughts

How I Adore Him

Joseph –
A Man of Notable Character
(Part 2)

By Kelly Byrley

Then Joseph her husband, being a just man, and not willing to make her a publick example, was minded to put her away privily.

Matthew 1:19

We will continue to study the character of Joseph during this uncertain time in his life.

Just

Matthew 1:19 calls Joseph a just man. Just means "righteous, innocent, and equitable." He lived righteously. He was fair. When he had considered writing Mary a bill of divorcement, he was planning to do it in secret to be fair to Mary. He wasn't cruel or unkind and he genuinely loved her. (Further reading: Psalm 106:3, Proverbs 20:7, Proverbs 31:9, James 3:17, Psalm 119:69.)

Discreet

We find Joseph's discretion in Matthew 1:19. He didn't want to make an example out of Mary. He didn't want her to have to face the public humility and shame that came with being adulterous and divorced. That was somethinxg that would stay with her forever, and he wanted to lessen the blow as much as possible. (Further reading: Proverbs 10:12, Proverbs 10:19, Proverbs 5:2.)

Compassionate

Joseph's compassion is clear in Matthew 1:19. He didn't want to publicly divorce Mary, and he certainly didn't want to have her stoned. Even if he thought she was guilty of a crime, he wasn't going to allow her to be punished. He would not stand by and watch the love of his life face public humiliation and die a cruel death. (Further reading: 1 Peter 4:8-9, Jude 22, Colossians 3:12-14.)

Selfless

Joseph set aside his own desires in Matthew 1:25 for the sake of others. I am sure that it was hard for him not to consummate his marriage, but he put his own needs and wants aside for the sake of Mary and for the sake of all people. The Bible was clear that baby Jesus would be born of a virgin. That meant Mary had to remain a virgin until after the birth. (Further reading: Ephesians 4:1-3, James 4:10, Philippians 4:11-13, Philippians 2:1-8.)

Brave

Joseph must have been afraid because in Matthew 1:20 the angel tells him not to fear. I am sure this was a terrifying time in Joseph's life. He's just a carpenter trying to live for the Lord and now he's faced with all of these crazy, overwhelming, incredible, yet scary responsibilities. I can't even imagine how overwhelming all of that was for him, from facing the gossip to raising the Saviour of the world. Oh, and let's not forget there were people trying to kill baby Jesus. The fear must have been crippling at times; yet, he overcame it, and he chose to walk by faith. (Further reading: Psalm 23:4, John 14:17, Psalm 56:3-4, Deuteronomy 31:6.)

Obedient

Every time the angel visited Joseph in Matthew 1-2, he obeyed immediately — from being told to take Mary as his wife, to naming the baby "Jesus," to packing up his family and moving. He did all of that without questioning, hesitating, or arguing. He simply trusted the Lord and obeyed. (Further reading: Acts 5:29, Psalm 119:30-35, Psalm 119:55-60, James 1:22-25.)

Faithful

Joseph was a carpenter; Jesus became a carpenter. Jesus is called the son of a carpenter in Mark 6:3. Joseph clearly spent a lot of time teaching Jesus the trade as all earthly fathers did with their sons. We also find them worshipping as a family in Luke 2. Joseph stayed committed to his family and to His Lord. He never left the path God had for him. (Further reading: Proverbs 3:5-6, Hebrews 10:23, Matthew 25:21.)

As Joseph was striving to live righteously, he had no idea what the Lord had planned for his future. He most likely lived like we all do: moment by moment, decision by decision, day by day. Through those everyday decisions, his standard of living caused the Lord to notice him. Joseph was faithful. He trusted the Lord. He obeyed, even when it went against common sense. He wasn't controlled by fear or his temper. He was a fair, patient, wise man who allowed the Lord to choose his path for him. He didn't stray. He didn't try doing things his own way. These qualities are all that any godly man should possess. They aren't limited to Joseph. Our sons should possess these and our daughters and single ladies should look for these in their potential future mates. In today's culture of weak, fearful, and emasculated males, can you only imagine the impact a generation of Josephs could have?

COME LET US Adore Him

Thoughts

How I Adore Him

How Should A King Come?

By Larissa Bell

For unto you is born this day in the city of David a Savior, which is Christ the Lord. And this shall be a sign unto you; Ye shall find the babe wrapped in swaddling clothes, lying in a manger.

Luke 2:11-12

"How Should a King Come" was a favorite Christmas song of my pastor in Bible college, and he would have the campus choir sing every year. I don't recall ever hearing it before my freshman year, but ever since the first time I heard it, I have thought of it often during the Christmas season. Its dynamic music score reminds me of a Rogers and Hammerstein movie, and the climactic ending gives me goosebumps just like listening to Handel's Messiah.

The first verse of the song talks about how everyone, even children, knows that the arrival of royalty should be accompanied by much fanfare, cheering crowds, and the finest transportation. Maybe it's the fairy tales we've heard since childhood that feed these expectations, or it could be the plethora of magazine covers at our grocery stores that want to share everything they can about Britain's royal family or celebrities that give us these ideas. But God chose a different way for His only Son to make an entrance into this world. A commoner was chosen to give birth to this special King of Kings in a stable. Later in life, Jesus chose a humble donkey to provide His ride into Jerusalem. Man's wisdom says royalty and celebrities need to be exalted by the people. God's wisdom teaches servant leadership and allows God to do the exalting (John 13:4-6, James 4:10).

The second verse then goes on to say that everyone, even commoners, knows that a king's purpose should be to accumulate wealth, treasures, and land. They should dine on the finest foods, wear the best clothes, and sleep in luxury. With our materialistic culture, we could easily interchange "king" with "I" in these expectations, couldn't we? Everywhere we turn, we're being assaulted with messaging that is the opposite of Matthew 6:33 where Scripture tells us to seek first the kingdom of God. A recent ad on my phone had a catchy jingle – "shop like a billionaire," while it displayed several items it thinks I should buy for myself. The problem is, I'm not a billionaire! A recent McDonald's ad goes so far as to tell me repeatedly during the 30-second spot that I deserve a steak patty on my breakfast sandwich. Can you spot these frequent lies of the devil in the world around you?

We don't deserve anything except an eternity in hell due to our sins. Yet, God, in His great love and mercy, sent His perfect Son to be our Savior and then graciously blesses our lives with everything we need (Philippians 4:19). The devil would love nothing more than to have Christians caught up in foolishly spending their money, time, and energy on the things of this world rather than giving God His tithes, supporting faith promise missions, spreading the gospel, and serving in church ministries. Remember that Jesus is the reason for this season. As Dave Ramsey says, "Don't buy things we don't need with money we don't have to impress people we don't like."

The final verse of this beautiful Christmas song describes the humble account of how the greatest King of all Kings made His entrance into this world. In a lowly manger, on a quiet night in Bethlehem, Jesus arrived with no fanfare, no crowds cheering, no fancy transportation, and no silk bed sheets. Philippians 2:7 tells us that Jesus left the perfect and beautiful Heaven to become a commoner on earth. He took on the form of a servant: going through the sufferings we go through (way more suffering than I have ever had to bear!) to give us an example of how we can also live victoriously over sin in this wicked world (Hebrews 4:15).

When was the last time you just sat in awe of all that God has done for mankind throughout history to show His love, mercy, grace, and countless other perfect attributes? It's incredibly humbling to think of God being willing to do all He has done despite our failures, sin, pride, apathy, rebellion, and ungratefulness. David said in Psalm 144:3, "Lord, what is man, that thou takest knowledge of him! Or the son of man, that thou makest account of him!" Psalm 103 has many verses about God's mercy and grace and how He knows us and loves us anyway. Make your reflection even more personal by remembering your salvation testimony and the innumerable ways God has blessed you spiritually, physically, and financially – we're just a speck of dust in the span of time, but He loves us like we're His only child!

Finally, the song ends by describing the angels singing "Glory, glory to God." Earth and mankind were silent for this miraculous appearance of the King that night; so, God sent the angels to bring the fanfare and cheering. While the angels got to fulfill this role 2,000 years ago, they certainly don't have to be the only ones worshipping and giving adoration to our King Jesus now. May we all take some time this Christmas season to listen to the words of all the beautiful Christmas hymns and think about how our King came – and may we give Him the glory He deserves this Christmas season and all year long!

COME LET US Adore Him

Thoughts

How I Adore Him

When Christmas Doesn't Look the Same

By Rainy Lehman

And Mary said, Behold the handmaiden of the Lord: be it unto me according to thy word. And the angel departed from her.

Luke 1:46-47

For twenty-five years of my life, Christmas looked exactly the same every single year. We woke up early on Christmas morning. My younger sister and I would assess the presents under the tree – yes, we did this even as adults – and we would wait excitedly for our parents to finally wake up, get their coffee, and meet us around the tree. I am convinced that no one pours coffee slower than my daddy on Christmas morning! We went one by one, opening our gifts, and then we always had the most delicious biscuits and gravy. Afterward, we would go to my grandmother's house to celebrate with her and my dad's family. It was a magical tradition that I loved and found comfort in.

Fast forward to today. I am a happily married Army wife! I am getting to live the desire of my heart with the man of my dreams, and I love this life that God has given me! However, anyone who has ever served in the military or married into military life knows that you get very little say in where you live and even where you spend your free time. On top of that, my husband is also an incredible physician, and medicine never takes a holiday. This past Christmas we got his December schedule and sure enough "Lehman" was listed as working on the 25th. With that information in hand, I began to wonder what Christmas was going to look like. One thing I knew for sure, it would not look the same.

I wish I could say that I took that revelation like a champ but much to my chagrin, I immediately began planning my pity party. I cannot go back and change last Christmas; all I can do is learn from it. Here are a few things I learned:

Despite the circumstances surrounding Christmas, the meaning of Christmas does not change! As simple as that may sound, when the traditions you are used to are no longer there, the devil will start to put thoughts in your mind like, "Well, Christmas is ruined – might as well not even celebrate it!" What a selfish thought! The perfect, holy Son of God willingly wrapped Himself in flesh and came down to earth for the sole purpose of saving a bunch of wretched, wicked, sinners like us! Jesus' birth is worth celebrating (Matthew 1:21)!

Make new traditions! Traditions to me mean safety and security, but when you no longer have those, a whole world of new possible traditions opens up to you. This year, my husband and I decorated cookies together for the first time, and we had a blast! We put cocoa in the thermos, loaded up our dogs, and went and drove through Christmas lights together. These are things that we probably would not have had time for if we had been away for the holidays, but these are precious memories that I will cherish forever.

Take a deep breath – it is all going to work out! I worried for weeks about this "new Christmas" because I did not know what to expect. Looking back, that was a lot of precious time and energy wasted on worrying. Sure, my heart was saddened a little when I had to watch my family open gifts together through a grainy video call, but my husband and I had the sweetest little Christmas. We got to spend some much-needed quality time together because we were not rushing from one family Christmas gathering to another or bombarded with friends' Christmas party invitations.

Christmas will be as special as you make it. If you are determined to have a pity party and not enjoy the wonder of the season, then that is exactly what you are going to have. You have the choice to make the best of the situation God has placed you in. So, I encourage you not to squander it.

I think about Mary, the mother of Jesus. Her Christmas looked vastly different than what she had planned. She did not plan to be a pregnant virgin and face the ridicule and shame that followed. She did not plan to make a long, uncomfortable journey while she was "great with child." Mary did not expect to give birth to the Son of God, let alone have to do it in a smelly manger. When the angel came to tell her the news, she had no idea what was awaiting her on this journey, but she placed her full trust in God and answered simply, "Behold the handmaid of the Lord; be it unto me according to thy word" (Luke 1:38).

There are missionaries, deployed soldiers, and people with spouses or children in Heaven. Christmas doesn't even feel like Christmas to them anymore. No matter what your situation, if Christmas looks a little different this year, let me challenge you to not get wrapped up in the negative. The traditions and plans are not what make Christmas Christmas. No matter how many gifts are under the tree, who is missing from around the dinner table, or where God has us this season, may we all be like Mary and be quick to reply, "Behold the handmaid of the Lord; be it unto me according to thy word."

COME LET US Adore Him

Thoughts

How I Adore Him

God's Christmas Plan

By Breanna Patton

Matthew 1:18-25, Luke 1:26-38

Christmas. What's the first thing that comes to mind when you hear the word "Christmas"? Most people think of Christmas parties, family get-togethers, Christmas music, general holiday cheerfulness, and other fun activities. But my mind cannot help but think of the young Mary and Joseph. What were their thoughts going into that first "Christmas season"?

Let's first look at Mary. Mary, I'm sure had been looking forward to the coming of the Lord and knew that Jesus was to be born of a virgin. Isaiah 7:14 says, "Therefore the Lord himself shall give you a sign; Behold a virgin shall conceive, and bear a son, and shall call him Immanuel." She must have known of the prophecy, yet how scared she must have been when the angel told her that she would be the virgin. (During this time, if it was found out that one was with child out of wedlock, she would be killed.) What were Mary's thoughts after the angel's visit? What emotions must she have been feeling? Was she scared, excited, nervous? I would have to assume maybe all three.

I am sure her first thoughts were of her unborn baby, not fully knowing what the future would hold for her and her child. No part of scripture says that she was upset or angry about what was going to happen, which tells me she must have loved the Lord and trusted Him with her unknown situation. Luke 1:38 says, "And Mary said, Behold the handmaid of the Lord; be it unto me according to thy word. And the angel departed from her." This verse tells us that she humbly accepted God's will. Would we humbly accept this news or would many of us question and complain stubbornly to the Lord?

Let's now look at Joseph. Matthew 1:19 says, "Then Joseph her husband, being a just man, and not willing to make her a public example, was minded to put her away privily. But while he thought on these things, behold, the angel of the LORD appeared unto him in a dream, saying, Joseph, thou son of David, fear not to take unto thee Mary thy wife: for that which is conceived in her is of the Holy Ghost." These verses show us that Joseph was not hasty in making a decision in regards to Mary. He waited and thought about what to do. Then, the angel of the Lord came and told him not to be fearful, that Mary was telling him the truth and the long awaited prophecy was going to be fulfilled through Mary.

When I think of the Christmas story, I am amazed at the gracious and humble spirits of both Mary and Joseph. The angel of the Lord came to each of them and explained God's plan for them, and they submissively accepted it. Too often when the Lord tells us what His plan is for us, we question Him because that is not our plan for our lives. We can't force our will and plans to happen when we want them to happen. You will be much more happy and content doing things God's way if you will only trust Him.

COME LET US Adore Him

Thoughts

How I Adore Him

God Chooses to Use Small

By Lydia L. Riley

And Mary said, My soul doth magnify the Lord, And my spirit hath rejoiced in God my Saviour. For he hath regarded the low estate of his handmaiden: for, behold, from henceforth all generations shall call me blessed. For he that is mighty hath done to me great things; and holy is his name.

Luke 1:46-48

The Bible is full of stories of how our great and mighty God chooses and uses the small and obscure. In bringing His very own Son into this world in human form, He chose that a woman would be the one to bear and deliver the greatest gift to mankind. Mary was young; Jewish history places her age somewhere between twelve to sixteen years old. She was simply a young girl, yet God chose her. He chose the "small" to bring His very best, His crowning work of redemption, into this sinful world.

He uses the small to show His power! Then, He receives the glory!

God uses small people, and God uses small places. He chose Bethlehem for the birth of His Son. Micah 5:2, "But thou, Bethlehem Ephratah, though thou be little among the thousands of Judah, yet out of thee shall he come forth unto me that is to be ruler in Israel...." God delights in using the seemingly overlooked, the little and despised, to bring about His most wondrous works.

God chose to send Heaven's best, the Creator and Ruler of the universe, in a very small, frail, and completely dependent little body. Our Saviour, Jesus Christ, not only chose to take on human flesh, but He chose to come within a small womb and be delivered in the smallest form of mankind – He chose to come as a baby, a baby born in a stable. God chose the small to accomplish His very best and most significant work in our universe. Be careful not to get so enamored and caught up with the world's importance placed on the "big" things that you begin to despise the day of "small things" for that is where God chooses to do His most mighty acts (Zechariah 4:10).

What is it in your life that seems so small and insignificant? Do you feel that perhaps the little tasks of tending to your little home and family are completely unnoticed by our Saviour? (Remember that God crowned motherhood with His divine plan in allowing only a woman to be able to bear children; this was His mighty plan of redemption!)

Do you wonder if your faithfulness in attending and ministering at your small church is even important? Our God loves to use the small things; never forget that! "But God hath chosen the foolish things of the world to confound the wise, and God hath chosen the weak things of the world to confound the things which are mighty;" I Corinthians 1:27.

Has God laid a thought on your heart that He is asking you to accomplish? Are you ashamed to share with others because it seems so small and unimportant? A smile, a meal, a word spoken from the heart – these are the "little" things that often set a life apart for God's glory and accomplish "big" things when done in His name! Think of the little lad with his little lunch when you begin to doubt what God can do with your "small" thing that you place in His hands!

Choose to believe God! Choose to give everything you have – no matter how small it may seem – give it all to Him! Watch Him make your "little" enough and accomplish His plan and His very best in your life. He is a God of miracles. He uses the small to show His power! Then, He receives the glory!

Luke 1:45, "And blessed is she that believed: for there shall be a performance of those things which were told her from the Lord."

COME LET US Adore Him

Thoughts

How I Adore Him

The Highly Favoured Hard Life

By Deborah South

And in the sixth month the angel Gabriel was sent from God unto a city of Galilee, named Nazareth, to a virgin espoused to a man whose name was Joseph, of the house of David; and the virgin's name was Mary. And the angel came in unto her, and said, Hail, thou that art highly favoured, the Lord is with thee: blessed art thou among women.

Luke 1:26-28

When I read the Christmas story, I try to consider the thoughts that Mary must have had. She was just a young, virgin girl waiting for her wedding day. I can imagine the excitement that filled her heart every time she saw Joseph. Mary was a pure girl ready to give her groom a pure bride. And then her life got hard! The angel Gabriel gave her the message that she would have Jesus, and that she was highly favoured! How could this be? What would people think? This was a troubling announcement to Mary.

She humbly watched Jesus do miracles that only God could do!

As I think of Mary, I think about the many things that she faced in her life. Some could even say, "Mary lived a hard life!" They would say her life was hard because she had to face the doubts that people would have about whether she was truly a virgin or not. Even Joseph questioned this. In his love for her, he did not want her to be embarrassed so he "being a just man, and not willing to make her a publick example, was minded to put her away privily."

Her life was hard because she, as a sinful soul, would be raising the sinless Son of God, Who "was in all points tempted like as we are, yet without sin" Hebrews 4:15b. As the songwriter said, "The wonder of wonders as she looked down and smiled that He was her Maker as well as her child. He created the womb that had given Him birth. He was God incarnate come down to the earth."

Her life was hard when she went to the wedding in Cana, and they ran out of wine. I wonder if maybe she had helped with the preparations. So when she was made aware that the wine was gone, she simply said to Jesus, "They have no wine."

Her life was hard when they led Jesus to Calvary, and she could do nothing but watch. Her life was hard when Jesus was on the cross and told John, "Behold thy mother! And from that hour that disciple took her unto his own home."

Her life was hard on the third day after the crucifixion as she made her way to the garden tomb holding the spices that she would put on the lifeless body of Jesus. She knew a heavy stone was in front of the tomb. It was going to be hard to move the stone.

Yes, Mary lived a hard life by the standard of the world. But what did Mary do with the situations mentioned above from her hard life?

She went to her cousin Elisabeth to rejoice with her in the miracles of two new babies (John the Baptist and Jesus) both coming in very strange situations! (Mary was a virgin, and Elisabeth was in her old age.)

She did her job with joy in raising Jesus and pondering the many things in her heart because of His life. She humbly watched Jesus do miracles that only God could do! She submitted to allowing a friend (the disciple, John) to be her help as she grew older. She saw the stone was moved away and Life had come forth!

Many of us can say at times that we have a hard life. How are you using the "hard" things in your life to allow God to be magnified and to realize how "highly favoured" you are?

COME LET US Adore Him

Thoughts

How I Adore Him

Home for the Holidays

By Nicole Redmon

"And she brought forth her firstborn son, and wrapped him in swaddling clothes, and laid him in a manger; because there was no room for them in the inn."

Luke 2:7

Ah! That phrase sure does have a nice ring to it, doesn't it? Being home for the holidays is something that we all strive for I do believe. There is nothing like being at Mama's house for Christmas or Granny's house for Christmas Eve or vice versa. The hustle and bustle of the season is just exciting to me. I know at times it can get a little tricky trying to figure out how to fit in all the festivities, but once your missions are complete, there is nothing like settling down in your own home!

Home. What does that word mean? Home is not just the four walls of your house trimmed out with garland and little lights that twinkle. Home is more than that. It's a feeling, an idea! Home can be anywhere that your heart is. There is truly no place like it! We have all heard the cute little sayings about the "home." We even put up little signs around our house that make us pause and think about how precious this place is that we call "Home." You can be at home across town or around the world from where you live.

Your home doesn't have to be "Pinterest perfect" to be a loving place. It just has to have Christ in the midst.

You can take your home with you everywhere you go. Home is what you make of it! And for the Christmas season, you can have a great holiday with friends and family in your "home."

There may be times throughout the holiday season when you get a little homesick. I know this is true for our family. We could sit around and pout and cry about not being with our family and church family, or we could be thankful for the time that the Lord has allowed us to have on the mission field. I bet even our Lord Jesus Christ must have felt homesick every now and then. I mean, He only left Heaven to come to this sin-cursed world to save us from our sins. He didn't even have a place to call home! Matthew 8:20 says, "And Jesus saith unto him, The foxes have holes, and the birds of the air have nests; but the Son of man hath not where to lay his head."

But just like He was reunited with His Heavenly Father, there will be times when we will gather again with our loved ones. Can you imagine the reunion day up in Heaven and how wonderful that time will be? It will be more exciting than any get-together down here! Are you missing certain people or places this Christmas? It is okay if you are. Pour your heart out to the Lord and ask Him to help you not to be lonely during the holidays. You can imagine Mary might have been a bit lonely in a stable far from home on the night she gave birth to baby Jesus.

But just like the stable that night was filled with heavenly love, make sure the home that you will be in for the holidays is filled with love! Christ's love. One hope that I have for my kiddos is that when they grow up and leave our home, they are filled with memories of a good holiday season around the house. I pray that they can look back on Christmas times in their childhood home and say that they may not have had everything that they ever wanted, but they knew that Dad and Mom loved them and each other so much and that Christ was the center of each holiday.

Teach your babies how to love, even on the hard days when it doesn't come so easily. Let them know how important it is to be thankful for the home that the Lord has provided for them. "Decorate" your home for the holidays with love, joy, peace, longsuffering, gentleness, meekness, temperanance goodness, and faith (Galatians 5:22-23). Not just the pretty things we find in the stores. Your home doesn't have to be "Pinterest perfect" to be a loving place. It just has to have Christ in the midst.

I'll leave you with this thought – our home for the holiday just might be in glory this year! Wouldn't that be wonderful?! Our earthly homes pale in comparison to the mansion that the Lord has gone to prepare for us! John 14:2, "In my Father's house are many mansions: if it were not so, I would have told you. I go to prepare a place for you."

You must be one of His to be in that home. John 3:7 says, "Marvel not that I say unto thee, ye must be born again." A true, personal relationship with Jesus Christ will guarantee you that home. A home where there will be no more sorrow or troubles or trials. We will forever be with our Savior. And that, my friend, is the home we should all be longing for.

COME LET US Adore Him

Thoughts

How I Adore Him

Two Kings – King Herod and King Jesus

By Makayla Fehr

"Saying, Where is he that is born King of the Jews? for we have seen his star in the east, and are come to worship him."
Matthew 2:2

Christmastime can mean a lot of different things for many people, especially those who are unsaved. One thing that always comes to my mind is how selfish people can be during this time of year. Yes, there are many who are extra generous, kind, and giving, but without fail, our human nature tends to be on the selfish side of wanting more or thinking we need more than what we already have! As I think about our Savior, selflessly born in a manger to die on the cross to save us, I think about the two kings we find in our Christmas story (Matthew 2:1-12).

Herod was an extremely selfish king:

1. **He was demanding.**

    "And when he had gathered all the chief priests and scribes of the people together, he demanded of them where Christ should

There is no one

who has sacrificed

or given us more

in this life

than Jesus Christ!

be born," Matthew 2:4. So many times in the Christian life, we feel we should have more or deserve something better, demanding more from those around us. It is so easy to be caught up thinking about how much more we deserve.

2. He was deceptive.

"Then Herod, when he had privily called the wise men, enquired of them diligently what time the star appeared," Matthew 2:7. It is sad that even as Christians we can become deceptive. It's easy to put on a good appearance in church or in front of the right people, but who are we behind closed doors and in our own home?

3. He was diligent in his own cause.

"And he sent them to Bethlehem and said, Go and search diligently for the young child..." Matthew 2:8a. It amazes me how when we want or need something just how diligently we search for the right deal or gift. But when it comes to our Christian life, we slack off. We are not as diligent in prayer and reading our Bible and being the witness we should be.

4. He was destructive.

"...for Herod will seek the young child to destroy him... Then Herod, when he saw that he was mocked of the wise men, was exceeding wroth, and sent forth, and slew all the children that were in Bethlehem..." Matthew 2:13;16. How destructive we can be with our words and actions towards others (not physically, but spiritually and emotionally)!

5. He was dead.

"But when Herod was dead..." Matthew 2:19a. Centuries later, we are still talking about King Herod and everything evil he did, but that is it. He died, and all we know about him are the negative things he did. How will we be remembered when we die?

Jesus Christ was an extremely selfless King. We see it all through scripture how Christ is.

1. He was and is always giving.
2. He was and is always truthful.
3. He was and is always seeking the best for others.
4. He was and is always helping.
5. He was and is still on the throne today.

There is no one who has sacrificed or given us more in this life than Jesus Christ! We are to be more Christlike every day. So this Christmas season. Let's try our best to become more like Him and less like King Herod.

COME LET US
Adore Him

Thoughts

How I Adore Him

The Most Wonderful Time of the Year

By Kate Ledbetter

Let this mind be in you, which was also in Christ Jesus: who, being in the form of God, thought it not robbery to be equal with God; but made himself of no reputation, and took upon him the form of a servant, and was made in the likeness of men: and being found in fashion as a man, he humbled himself, and became obedient unto death, even the death of the cross.

Philippians 2:5-8

Christmas is a magical time of the year. Since I was a child, I have loved the transformation our lives went through. We decorated differently; we sang different songs; we dressed in festive clothes; and we gave each other a special consideration that just didn't seem to exist the rest of the year. For me, this selflessness that comes once a year is the most reflective thing I see in the Christmas story.

Many people argue that Jesus could not have been born in December. They are most likely right. I've known a few people who won't participate in the holiday season citing its pagan roots. That is fine if that's all they can see. But when I look at Christmas, I can't help but think of these verses: Philippians 2:5-8.

I celebrate Christmas because:

1. Of its emphasis on Christ. Because Christmas starts with Christ, I will celebrate.

2. Of those who hate Christ. They strive to leave Him out. Atheists and pagans won't call it Christmas. They replace Christ with an "X."

3. In the mind of Christ, Jesus took on the form of a servant and gave us the gift of Himself. This time of the year, let me lay down more of myself as I serve others.

4. The birth of Christ deserves to be celebrated even if it's on the wrong day.

We take the time to celebrate so many events these days. We celebrate birthdays, anniversaries, special occasions, and other holidays. I hope we take the time to worship the Lord every day. I hope that He gets far more than just a holiday. I am going to do extra for the holiday though! I'm going to choose to go all out to celebrate Jesus' choice to leave Heaven and take on the form of a man to lay down His life for mine. I won't let that opportunity to celebrate be wasted. It's the most wonderful time of the year!

COME LET US
Adore Him

Thoughts

How I Adore Him

Growing with God

By Cherith Shiflett

And the angel came in unto her, and said, Hail, thou that art highly favoured, the Lord is with thee: blessed art thou among women. And when she saw him, she was troubled at his saying, and cast in her mind what manner of salutation this should be. And the angel said unto her, Fear not, Mary: for thou hast found favour with God.

Luke 1:28-30

Have you ever heard a message and you just knew the words would ring in your head for years to come? I heard a message preached in July and it was definitely one of those messages! It just happened to be about Mary and her highly-favoured life. When I was asked to write for this devotional, I second-guessed myself a few times because it wouldn't be 100% original and it seemed cliché to the series (just like the devil to get in your head, huh?) but the more I prayed and studied, I was convinced this was it!

I think it's safe to say, Mary was growing with God- quite literally! Let's look at some things in Mary's life that will help us Grow with God.

1. Her Persuasion

In the Bible days, names meant something. They were given with the future in mind or according to what was happening at that time. For example, Moses' name meant "to pull out/draw out of water." So, what does Mary mean? Surely it means sweet, pure, and humble, right? Her name actually comes from the Hebrew word that means "rebellious or bitter." That doesn't sound like the Mary we know. I think we can agree that somewhere along the line there had to be a decision on Mary's part. Mary was a girl, born into a sinful generation, just like me and you, but there was a persuasion that took place in her life. She went from being this bitter, rebellious young person to being the one that God would use to bring His Son into the world! At some point in your life, there needs to be a record of a change. We are born into sin and rebellion. If you choose to accept Christ, that evokes a change. When God changes you, you're no longer identified by your past. All He sees is a vessel for His use.

2. Her Purity

There is no debate according to the scriptures that Mary was a virgin (vs. 27). If you're going to grow with God, there will have to be a time in your life when your purity becomes a priority. This will have to be a decision you are dedicated to, something you factor into your life. Purity requires a conscious decision.

Mary was growing with God, and she was focused on her purity. It's not popular or easy, but it is right. Make purity a priority in every aspect of your life. Philippians 4:8 - "Finally, brethren, whatsoever things are true, whatsoever things are honest, whatsoever things are just, whatsoever things are pure, whatsoever things are lovely, whatsoever things are of good report; if there be any virtue, and if there be any praise, think on these things."

If you have any desire to grow with God, you must make purity a priority. Live clean. Live right according to God's standards.

3. Her Process

This is probably my favorite part. Verse 28 says, "And the angel came in unto her, and said, Hail, thou that art highly favored, the Lord is with thee: blessed art thou among women."

Highly favoured means "to grace, to endue with special honor, to make accepted or highly favored." The angel is telling Mary, "Mary, you are highly favored. God has chosen you. God has his eyes on you. God has picked you out."

Like Mary, God has picked you out. You are highly favored! I think the devil has tried to convince us that if we decide to grow with God, if we commit to purity, then we are taking a step back. He tries to convince us of all the things we are going to miss out on.

If you go with God, stick to the commitments you've made, and decide to grow with God, you are highly favoured.

The God of Heaven wants to talk to you. He wants to be your all in all. He stirs your heart. He speaks to you, convicts you, guides you, blesses you, loves you (and the list could go on and on). All these are signs we are highly favoured.

We're not missing out; we're not taking a step back. God has His eye on you, and He's selected you for service - not the young person who has all the adults fooled or the woman who never takes the things of God seriously. He selected you with something in your heart that desires to grow in God. You, who says I think God wants to do something in my life, but I can't imagine Him using little ole' me. You, refusing to give up your beliefs, even surrounded by people who doubt God. Just like Mary, you are highly favoured.

I think we can learn so much about growing with God through the life of Mary. She was unknown and insignificant; she was doubted and criticized by others, but Mary was highly favoured by God and blessed among women.

It all started with her being willing to grow with God. May we follow Mary's example in growing with God and living that highly favoured life.

COME LET US Adore Him

Thoughts

How I Adore Him

Christmas Joy

By Renee Patton

Now therefore thus saith the Lord of hosts; Consider your ways.

Haggai 1:5

I love Christmas! Family time, hot chocolate, baking cookies, fun excursions, and gift giving. Then there's the smell of cinnamon pine cones sweet Christmas carols playing in the store, and the lights – all the beautiful Christmas lights! Who doesn't love Christmas, right? Well, some may not. Christmas may be a very negative time for some. We are all moved by our previous experiences, whether good or bad, and sometimes we choose to break the cycle.

Christmas brings a coziness of Christ, love, and peace. These are emotions, yes; however, humanity is built on emotion. The key is how we use our emotions to live and serve the Lord. Negative events in our lives will bring negative emotions. While we need time to grieve, endure, or whatever it may be, joy will come

That warm, fuzzy feeling of Christmas joy is a choice.

in the morning (Psalms. 30:5b). We must sift through our circumstances and find joy. If not, bitterness may take root and defile our spirit (Hebrews 12:15).

On the contrary, positive events bring positive emotions. Our hearts thrive on joy! Joy is a good medicine. Look at Proverbs 17:22, "A merry heart doeth good like a medicine: but a broken spirit drieth the bones." This is a wonderful verse relating joy and heartbreak to our physical wellbeing.

Some time ago, the phrase "Consider your ways" (Haggai 1:5b) stayed with me for days after my Bible reading. Every single day I have thought about my ways. My ways have brought joy to others; yet, they have also brought pain. I work very diligently to consider my ways; although, I am not always successful at decision-making or talking to another.

There have been many times in my life I have had to choose to break the cycle of negative circumstances. The greatest positive a negative situation can bring to you is empathy. I can now better understand what someone is going through when I have "already walked in similar shoes." I do not know what another is dealing with, going through, or hurting from, thus, learning to tread lightly with others will help me to consider my ways.

That warm, fuzzy feeling of Christmas joy is a choice – everyday – as we consider our ways.

Consider your ways...

    ...walk a little slower.

    ...talk a little kinder.

    ...be a little sweeter.

    ...show empathy – cry or pray with others when needed.

Christmas may have hurtful connotions for some while it may be the greatest time of the year for others. I pray that I may "consider my ways" so others may see that sweet, Christmas joy not only in December, but every single day.

While we travel these days of Christmas, may we consider our ways and be a blessing while bringing joy to others. As a Christian, we have received the ultimate Christmas gift from Christ – His Son – our salvation. May we give the gift of "considering our ways" and brightening someone else's Christmas this holiday season.

COME LET US Adore Him

Thoughts

How I Adore Him

The Gift That Keeps On Giving

By Bethany Riley

Jesus answered and said unto her, If thou knewest the gift of God, and who it is that saith to thee, Give me to drink; thou wouldest have asked of him, and he would have given thee living water.

John 4:10

One of my favorite parts about Christmas is the gift-giving. I love finding the perfect gift for my family and friends and watching their delighted faces as they open it. I like to give gifts that have a practical purpose. One of the first things I ask myself when Christmas shopping is, "They are charging *how much*?!" And then I ask, "Will they really use this?" or maybe, "Will this gift really make their life better?" Many of us already know that God gave us His Son (John 3:16) and have received the free gift of salvation. My challenge to you is to fully appreciate the gift we have in Jesus Christ. He is the ultimate gift that keeps on giving. He could have just saved us and then left us alone,

Jesus Christ - the ultimate gift that keeps on giving.

but the truth is that our salvation just keeps on getting better and better. Verse 14 of the same chapter talks about how the gift of God satisfies forever. I think about how wonderful my life is and how fulfilling serving God is. The only reason I get to enjoy my life with all the people in it and all its seasons (especially the Christmas Season!) is because God gave the most precious gift, our Savior. Here are some things that God has given me because I received Him:

Ecclesiastes 5:19, I Corinthians 10:31 - God gave me a purposeful existence. The very fact that I get to exist is a gift from God, and because I received the gift of Jesus Christ, I get to enjoy being alive! Because of Him, I can enjoy working, eating, and living on His provisions. Because of Him, I get to enjoy the delicious foods, memories with my family, and joy that Christmas brings.

John 4:18, 28-30 - God gave me a changed life. The woman at the well's life changed! She went from living a promiscuous lifestyle to telling her village about this Man who is Christ. Although my testimony is different from hers, my life changed as well. I shudder to think what my life would look like if I had not gotten saved at an early age, and I am so thankful for all the nasty scars I missed out on.

Philippians 4:6,7 - God gives me prayer and peace (the result of prayer). The gift of prayer has been so mighty in my life. I am so thankful I can take anything to im in prayer. The gift of peace that passeth all understanding is so sweet!

James 1:5 - God gives me wisdom. I don't know about you, but I am constantly in need of God's wisdom. God has been so gracious to give me the wisdom to face situations that I would normally mess up in my own "wisdom." When I don't know what to do, all I have to do is open God's Word. He'll give me the solution.

John 14:16, 26 - God gave me the Holy Spirit. The Holy Spirit guides me into truth. He helps me understand the scriptures that my brain can't seem to understand. He gives me clarity when I am not sure if something is "passable" or not. He whispers comfort.

I John 5:11 - God gave me eternal life. I get to enjoy heaven and all of its pleasures. I get to see all my loved ones who have already passed on. Not to mention the best part yet, I get to see my Savior face to face!

Romans 12:6, I Peter 4:10 - God gave me a spiritual gift to use for Him. Romans 12 lists the spiritual gifts. What is yours? I know I want to fulfill my role in the body of Christ and glorify Him with the gift He has given me.

This list is very basic and simply scratching the surface of everything our precious Savior gives us. When we receive a gift, our natural reaction is to give something back. We have received the wonderful gift of God; the least we can do is give our lives, love, and labor back to Him.

COME LET US Adore Him

Thoughts

How I Adore Him

Let Every Heart Prepare Him Room

By Callie Payne

And she brought forth her firstborn son, and wrapped him in swaddling clothes, and laid him in a manger; because there was no room for them in the inn.

Luke 2:7

"No room in the inn..." Imagine not even wanting to give up your own room for an expecting mother in labor. They may not have known who she was or who she was carrying, but it didn't seem to matter. Imagine being so full of self and wrapped up in what we want that we would miss such an opportunity. Sadly enough, this is what many of us do too often during a busy or difficult time in our lives. Many times when everything is going great, we push God off to the side as if we don't need Him.

What's your desire for this season? Do you desire special memories, thoughtful gifts, or sweet experiences? While none of those are bad things to want, I encourage you to weigh your desires.

This busy season of life could look different for everyone. Maybe you're running back and forth from church events or shopping for that perfect gift for someone you love. Maybe you feel like you can't catch a break from hosting holiday parties or other festive activities. Whatever the case, we all know why the Christmas season can start to feel overwhelming.

Check your heart this year. Have you prepared Him room? Sometimes you may have to plan ahead your personal time with Him each day.

What about as the new year approaches? Are you already making plans and preparing all of your goals? How about making some personal spiritual goals? How sad would it be if God wanted to move in your life in a huge way this season, but when He came to speak to your heart, you had no room for Him, no room for change, no room to listen. You're working on your "game plan" for the holidays and focused on all the things you "need" to get done.

Please take time to prepare your heart each day for Him to work. If He wanted to work in your life, would there be room for Him? Are you more concerned about keeping up with your plans or desiring His presence in your life?

COME LET US Adore Him

Thoughts

How I Adore Him

The Gift of the Present
(Part 1)

By Kathy Lane

Put on therefore, as the elect of God, holy and beloved, bowels of mercies, kindness, humbleness of mind, meekness, longsuffering; forbearing one another, and forgiving one another, if any man have a quarrel against any; even as Christ forgave you, so also do ye.

Colossians 3:12-13

It was another beautiful August night at New Hope Baptist Church. As the pastor approached the pulpit to deliver his Sunday evening message, he felt strongly led by the Holy Spirit to change what he was going to be preaching. In obedience to the Spirit's leading, he set his notes aside and began preaching from his heart to the congregation about taking the next step of faith in their walk with the Lord.

"Do you trust Him? Are you willing to do whatever it takes to step out in faith? I cannot keep carrying you — I cannot keep pleading with you to stop being fearful." As he began the invitation, he challenged those willing to allow God to do anything that He desired in their lives to step forward as a testimony to the Lord. Several came forward, including the tender-hearted pastor's wife — who had been serving faithfully with him for decades in ministry. At the end of the invitation, he encouraged the church family to act upon what the Lord had laid upon their hearts and not let fear hold them back.

We have no right whatsoever as a child of God to harbor a resentful or unforgiving spirit toward others.

The pastor went home that evening with his wife, went to sleep, and the next time he opened his eyes, he was in Heaven. He was wholeheartedly willing to allow God to use him however He saw fit, even if that meant he just preached his last message here on earth. That pastor was my father-in-law, Missionary Mike Lane to Honduras, and he unexpectedly passed away at sixty-three years old after serving the Lord in ministry his entire life.

Every year when the holiday season rolls around, it brings back so many bittersweet memories of "Dad-Dad Lane" (as the grandkids affectionately called him). As I was reminiscing on old family memories, it had me thinking about regrets as well – the "should have's" in life. We should have tried calling one more time ... We should have spent more time with them ... and the list could go on forever.

I thought of how many people have regrets when tragedy falls on a loved one, and they long to turn back time and change past choices. I thought about this Christmas season and the joy of our Saviour's birth, and how such a precious time of year could be filled with so much remorse with the "should have's" of times past. We know that our life here on earth is limited as James 4:14 states, "Whereas ye know not what shall be on the morrow. For what is your life? It is even a vapour, that appeareth for a little time, and then vanisheth away." As believers, we must not waste any time lamenting over the past and the numerous mistakes we have made, instead, we should be focusing on what God has for us today, right now, in the present. When my husband and I were working with the young couple's class at our home church, we had a sweet young couple dealing with family issues during the Christmas season. The husband was having difficulty forgiving his mother for events that happened long ago, and it was eating away at him year after year. After weeks of the Holy Spirit dealing with his heart, he called his mother and began mending the hurtful, bitter feelings and unforgiveness, and that relationship was slowly restored. He mentioned he wished he had not waited so long and that he "should have" done it years earlier.

What about us? Is there a seed of bitterness or unforgiveness in our hearts toward someone? I know that personally some of the worst hurts come from those closest to me—whether it be my physical or spiritual family. I can't help but think of the account in Matthew 18 where Jesus speaks to Peter about the king who had compassion and forgave his servant of all that he owed, and yet the servant (who had been forgiven of all his debt), would not extend the same compassion and forgiveness on his fellow servant.

Oftentimes a bitter heart cannot even recognize its own condition as it is overshadowed by its self-righteous pride. With every breath we take, we must be reminded of the very costly gift of salvation and unconditional love that our Saviour extends to us. We have no right whatsoever as a child of God to harbor a resentful or unforgiving spirit toward others when we have been wholly forgiven and freed from the condemnation and penalty of sin. Christ bore the full weight of the cross and became the atoning sacrifice to redeem us – the very ones guilty of putting Him there. Yet we still refuse to surrender the resentment in our hearts.

COME LET US Adore Him

Thoughts

How I Adore Him

The Gift of the Present
(Part 2)

By Kathy Lane

Therefore, my beloved brethren, be ye steadfast, unmoveable, always abounding in the work of the Lord, forasmuch as ye know that your labour is not in vain in the Lord.

I Corinthians 15:58

While living in Washington state, my husband and I frequently visited a hardware store close by and had been witnessing to a young employee named Ben for several years. We had given him the gospel message on multiple occasions and pleaded with him to come to church year after year. A few months ago, while we were on the mission field, we found out that he was in the hospital with Covid. We immediately contacted our home church and asked for a staff member to visit him. Unfortunately, at that time, the hospital was not allowing any visitors into the ICU. About a week later, we were informed that he died due to unforeseen complications with Covid. Ben was in his twenties, and this year his family will celebrate Christmas without him. We do not know if he accepted Christ before he passed, but we do know that he was given the gospel message very clearly on multiple occasions. We pray that he acted upon that before slipping into eternity. Thankfully, that is one situation in which we obeyed the Holy Spirit's leading instead of putting it off and shamefully adding another "should have" to our list.

During such a hectic time of year, we can easily become so caught up with the holidays that we overlook the souls God places in our pathway. Leading lost sinners to Christ should always be our topmost priority, and this is such an opportune season to creatively get the gospel out to those who may normally not be as receptive. Our family often puts together gift baskets with a Bible, an invitation from our church, candy canes, and other goodies to hand out during the holidays.

Who has the Lord specifically placed in your pathway for you to witness to this Christmas season? Your local first responders? City or state council members? The clerk at the grocery store? The neighbor who drives you crazy? We need to make sure we are attentively and purposefully listening to the Holy Spirit and not becoming guilty of leaving Christ out of Christmas!

Let us not forget this year to take some extra time each day in the stillness of our hearts to beg God to show us how He would have us spend not only this Christmas season but also the new year. I'm sure that each of us has a long list of regrets in our lifetime, but let's be determined this year to not allow another year to go by with more "should have's."

We cannot change the past, nor can we foresee the future, but we do have a choice to make a difference *now* — in the present. And what an amazing gift from God it is!

COME LET US Adore Him

Thoughts

How I Adore Him

It's a Wonderful Life!

By Debra Birner

When I was a child, I spake as a child, I understood as a child, I thought as a child: but when I became a man, I put away childish things.

1 Corinthians 13:11

Ahh, Christmas. Okay, you probably just read that verse and thought – that's not a "Christmas" verse! But I think my life can be defined by the Christmases in my life.

When I think about my early Christmases, I remember the fun traditions we had. I remember getting the tree, storing it in the cellarway, and then so carefully decorating it.

When I got married, Christmases were different. We had a big Christmas event at my mother-in-law's house every Christmas Eve and a Christmas gathering with my family on Christmas Day. As our children were growing up, I remember my excitement as I anticipated the children waking up and opening their gifts.

It seems each Christmas I recall, it reflects a different season in my life.

Up until 1999, Christmases were about family, traditions, good times, shopping, special treats – all good memories that I cherish, but it was different in 1999. That was the year I understood the gospel and received Christ as my Saviour. When Christmas came, it was more special than it had ever been. Because I had been born again that year, the birth of Jesus Christ was amazing in a way I never grasped before.

We still enjoyed celebrating with family and carrying on traditions, but now we had new traditions as well. I remember one year putting Bible verses on each gift and the children had to guess what the gift was with the "clue" from the Bible verse. We made some new traditions and we let some traditions go, as we felt those traditions didn't honor God.

One year, Christmas was on a Sunday. In that particular year, we ran a bus to church, my husband taught Sunday school, then we took the kids home on the bus, went to the nursing home where we had a Christmas service, then a quick meal and back to church for the evening service. After that, we all as a family went to the mission together. We had our holiday meal and gift exchanges on Christmas Eve that year in anticipation of a busy Christmas Day. I am thankful I was able to raise my children to know that Christmas is a time of year that we had fun, did some silly things, but that more importantly, we served the Lord.

I am in another season of life now. My children are grown and they all have children of their own. I love the song, "It's Different Now" – because Christmas before Christ was very different from Christmas after Christ. I am glad, as another song says, "I Know Who Jesus Is."

II Corinthians 5:17, Therefore if any man be in Christ, he is a new creature: old things are passed away; behold, all things are bviecome new.

COME LET US Adore Him

Thoughts

How I Adore Him

Will You Submit?

By Grace Shiflett

For I came down from heaven, not to do mine own will, but the will of him that sent me.

John 6:38

During this season, I just love reflecting on the birth of Christ. The amazing joy we feel as we realize Jesus left the perfection of Heaven to come down and dwell among men. We all should take time often to revisit the miraculous birth of our Saviour. He came to earth on our behalf to offer Himself so that we could be reconciled with the Father.

Do you ever stop to think of Jesus becoming flesh - not for His own will, but for the will of the One that sent Him? The example He set for us by living out the Father's will above His own will is incredible. We rejoice in His coming to earth because we can without a doubt see the many lives that are forever changed by Jesus living in the will of His Father.

Laying aside one's own will can be a challenge to the flesh. As we live our lives, there are times when our Heavenly Father will ask something of us, and it is at that moment that our will is put to the test.

When these times arise, may we have the strength to choose the will of our Father's leading. He knows best!

I remember a specific time in my life when I knew God was leading. My will was very strong, and I felt I knew a better way. I asked my husband if I could ask the Lord for what I wanted. I will never forget what he said to me. He said, "You can ask, but you need to end your prayer with 'not my will but thine be done.'" That was many years ago, and as I look back from this view, I'm thankful that I submitted to the will of the Father and not my own. He did know best, even though my flesh wanted what seemed to have been an easier path.

I challenge you today to follow the example Jesus set for us by walking in the will of the Father. It began at the manger, but led Him all the way to the cross where once again, He submitted to the will of the One that knows best. My life has changed because He laid aside His own will and came down for me.

Laying aside one's own will can be a challenge to the flesh.

COME LET US Adore Him

Thoughts

How I Adore Him

The Joy the Saviour Brought

By Rikki Beth Poindexter

And the angel said unto them, Fear not: for, behold, I bring you good tidings of great joy, which shall be to all people.
Luke 2:10

No one loves this time of the year more than I do! I love everything about it: celebrating the birth of the Saviour, decorations, music, food, smells, family time, special events, NC weather (which can mean anything – but I love the cold of winter). I truly love it all! As a homeschooling mom, we took two weeks off and enjoyed every minute of that break. I try to soak it all in ...not wishing it here faster, but when the season gets here, just trying to absorb it all.

I have heard others lament about the sad feeling of it when it is all over. I have felt that in years past: the mess that comes with all of the cooking; the chaos that opening both gifts and your home to guests brings; the untidiness of the home as more things come

Look for the joy the Saviour offers to us, not just at Christmas, but throughout the year!

to live there (aka toys); the time it takes to decorate (most of us don't mind decorating, it's the putting away that gets us). All of the work and labor that goes into the season, and just like that, it's over. I didn't have joy about the season; I had happiness in the season. Happiness is based on circumstances. Joy is not. Great joy came into the world the day the Saviour was born. Let joy be the dominant part of our celebrations.

In the last ten years, I have personally come to love the week from 12/26-1/2. I still consider this Christmas! I love the freshness of the new year. I love reflecting on what God has done that year, the prayers He has answered, the changes He has made in my life, and what He has done in and for our family. I love sitting in the quiet house early in the morning with my decorations still up (I'm one of those people) and my Bible and my prayer book (see the Highly Favoured Life Prayer devotional for more on that). There is much joy in this!

You see, the joy that the Saviour brought at His birth was meant to be present and enJOYed through the ages, not just in a season. The joy that He gives is everlasting! I have previously written about our Helpers of Joy: trust the Lord; focus on Him; be obedient; be content.

Time with family is wonderful. For the first time in my married life, my immediate family celebration will look different due to our daughter being married and living in another state.

That doesn't have to dictate my joy or lack thereof at this time of the year. I am so happy for my daughter and son-in-law!

I have lost close family members to death, so I do remember the sadness (no one can explain) at this time of the year. I seem to notice their absence more and feel the emptiness that death can bring more at this time of the year. This year, try to focus on the ones that are present, the ones you can reach out and touch. Look for the joy the Saviour offers to us, not just at Christmas, but throughout the year.

Keep Him at the beginning of everything you do during this wonderful season. Even if you do not love this time of the year as I do, you can still have joy. Look at and spend the week after Christmas differently this year. Don't dread it. Look forward to it with joy and anticipation!

The greatest gift of all was born, and it was joy to all people: the Saviour was born. The gift of joy!

COME LET US Adore Him

Thoughts

How I Adore Him

About The Authors

Each author has been handpicked because of their testimony for Christ. God has gifted each writer with incredibly versatile perspectives of the Christian life. These godly ladies come from all walks of life including pastor's wives and daughters, missionary wives, church staff ladies, and faithful church members. Their written words of wisdom are sure to bless your heart.

To know more about our writers please visit:
thehighlyfavouredlife.com/our-story

Salvation Made Simple
By Renee Patton

Admit. One must first admit they are a sinner. Romans 3:10 states, "As it is written, There is none righteous, no, not one." Sin is everywhere and we all commit sin, many times without even trying. Perhaps in a conversation, we say something innocently, then realize it was not correct. That, my friend, is lying. Of course, murder is a sin that is seen and felt by those affected. However, lying is too. Jeremiah reminds one that "The heart is deceitful above all things, and desperately wicked: who can know it?" (17:9). A baby does not have to be told how to sin, it is simply in our nature. One must admit they are a sinner otherwise we make God a liar as found in I John 1:10, "If we say that we have not sinned, we make him a liar, and his word is not in us."

Believe. One must believe Jesus came to this earth to be born and die for our sins. "For God so loved the world, that he gave his only begotten Son, that whosoever believeth in him should not peish, but have everlasting life" (John 3:16). God desires that we should not perish, thus the choice is ours. God gives man the opportunity for salvation if man would take it. Romans 5:8 states "But God commendeth his love toward us, in that, while we were yet sinners, Christ died for us." Webster's 1828 Dictionary defines commendeth as entrusts or gives. So, God gave us His love through His Son, Jesus. Furthermore, Romans 5:19 shows how sin came from Adam and is made righteous through Christ, "For as by one man's disobedience [Adam] many were made sinners [mankind], so by the obedience of one [Jesus] shall many [mankind] be made righteous."

Confess. Confession is made with one's own mouth. The words must come from the person alone. Romans 10:9 talks of both confession and believing, "That if thou shalt confess with thy mouth the lord Jesus, and shalt believe in thine heart that God hath raised him from the dead, thou shalt be saved." The key is I have to confess to God. My husband or friend cannot confess for me. While God gives man the opportunity on earth, there will be a time every knee will bow and confess God is Lord, "For it is written, As I live, saith the Lord, every knee shall bow to me, and every tongue shall confess to God" (Romans 14:11).

To see more resources on salvation visit:
https://www.thehighlyfavouredlife.com/simple-salvation

If you made this decision, please contact us at *highlyfavouredlife @gmail.com*. We would love to rejoice with you in the new life you now have in Christ.

Made in the USA
Columbia, SC
29 January 2025